SAINT JOSEPH

CTS Children's Books

Contents

Text by Francesca Fabris

Illustrations by Silvia Fabris

Translated by Pierpaolo Finaldi

Saint Joseph: Published 2012 by The Incorporated Catholic Truth Society, 40-46 Harleyford Road, London SE11 5AY. Tel: 020 7640 0042; Fax: 020 7640 0046; www.cts-online.org.uk. Copyright © 2012 The Incorporated Catholic Truth Society in this English-language edition.

ISBN: 978 1 86082 800 3   CTS Code CH 40

Translated from the original Italian Edition **San Giuseppe** - ISBN 978-88-6124-333-0, published by Il Pozzo di Giacobbe, Gruppo Editoriale S.R.L., Cortile San Teodoro, 3, 91100 Trapani (TP), Italy © 2012 Il Pozzo di Giacobbe.

A CARPENTER
FROM NAZARETH

Joseph was a very special person. Every child would have wanted him as a father. Before he became a dad, Joseph was all alone, looking for a girl to love. "I'll love my wife and my children more than anyone. And I'll protect them to the end!" he would say to himself whenever he thought about his future family. Joseph lived in a little town called Nazareth where everyone knew him well and loved him. He worked as a carpenter and was very skilled with saws, hammers, nails and all the tools that are used to build houses, furniture, doors and windows.

He was a descendant of King David, the most famous king of Israel spoken of in the scriptures. The prophets said that the Messiah, the son of God would be born of the house of David.

THE FLOWERING STAFF

One day when Joseph was in his workshop, news arrived from Jerusalem. Zechariah the priest was summoning all the unmarried young men of the royal house of David to the temple in Jerusalem. From among these men, God himself would choose a husband for a young woman named Mary.

Mary was a special girl. She was so special that every child would have wanted her as a mother. She was beautiful, good and gentle and as a child had lived and worked in the temple, praying all the time.

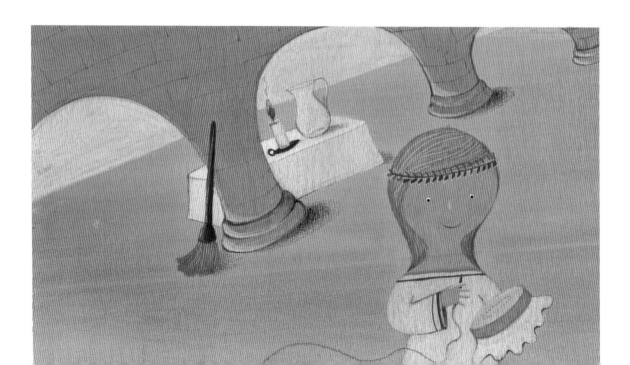

Joseph made his way to Jerusalem with the other young men of the house of David. Each man was told to bring the staff he carried for long journeys and God would send a sign to show which one he chose to be the husband of Mary. Zechariah the priest collected each young man's staff and brought them into the temple. He laid them on the altar and began to pray. Outside, a crowd had gathered, waiting to hear the good news. Joachim and

Anna - Mary's parents - waited with baited breath, holding each other's hands tight. Mary was also nervous and was waiting to see who God had chosen for her to share her life with.

At last, Zechariah came out of the temple with all the staffs and returned each one to its owner.

The last staff belonged to Joseph and by a miracle, white flowers had begun to grow from the top of the staff. Joseph had been chosen by God! Mary and Joseph looked tenderly into each other's eyes and fell in love. They were engaged immediately and promised to be married and to live in love and faithfulness for their whole life.

A MYSTERIOUS PREGNANCY

Many had tried to work out the time when the Messiah would come. Looking for clues in the words of the prophets or among the stars in the heavens. But the exact time of the birth of the son of God was a secret which God had kept to himself. After her engagement Mary went off to visit her cousin Elizabeth. Elizabeth was expecting a baby and Mary wanted to be near her to help her during her pregnancy. A few months later when she returned, Mary's own tummy had grown. She was also expecting a baby! Joseph was worried. He was not the father of the baby Mary had in her womb and he wasn't sure what to do. Should he break off their engagement or stay with Mary and look after her baby?

That night Joseph tossed and turned in his bed with a thousand thoughts in his head. As soon as he fell asleep the Angel of the Lord appeared to him in a dream and said: "Joseph do not be afraid of marrying Mary. The baby in her womb comes from God and you shall call him Jesus. He is the Messiah who has come to save his people from their sins. It was foretold through the prophets that a virgin would bear a son and his name would be Emmanuel, God with us!" When Joseph woke up, he did what the Angel told him to do. He married Mary, took her into his house and prepared everything for the arrival of the special baby that she carried within her.

IN BETHLEHEM

Mary's tummy had already grown very big when news of a census arrived in Nazareth. The Emperor wanted to know exactly how many people he ruled over, and all the people in Palestine were ordered to go and be counted in the town where they were born. Joseph's family was from Bethlehem so Mary and Joseph began the long journey from Nazareth to Bethlehem. Mary travelled on a donkey across the desert with Joseph. When they arrived in Bethlehem, Mary knew that it was almost time for the baby to be born. It was almost night and Joseph went from house to house and inn to inn asking for a room where the baby could be born.

There was no room for them anywhere! Many people had come to Bethlehem for the census and every inn was full. An Innkeeper told Joseph that they could stay in a stable where the animals were kept. It was warm and dry there at least.

So Jesus was born in a stable with his mother and father and an ox and a donkey. Mary wrapped the baby in swaddling clothes and let Joseph hold him tenderly. Joseph looked at Jesus with eyes full of love and held him close to his cheek. In his heart he said: "Yes, Lord my God, Blessed be your Holy Name! I promise to be your earthly father and look after you until you are ready to make your own way." Baby Jesus held Joseph's finger tight in his tiny hand.

SHEPHERDS AND SHEEP

While Mary and Joseph looked happily at Jesus who was so small and defenceless, some shepherds arrived and asked timidly: "what will you call this child?" "We will call him Jesus!" answered Joseph. "Then we have come to worship him!" said the oldest shepherd.

Joseph and Mary were amazed and could not understand why the shepherds had come. They then told the story of what had happened that night. They were sleeping in the fields watching over the sheep when suddenly they saw a bright light in the sky and an angel of God came down to them and said: "Do not be afraid I have come to bring you news of great joy! Today a saviour has been born for you, he is Christ the Lord. Go and you will find a baby wrapped in swaddling clothes and lying in a manger."

When the angel had finished speaking a multitude of angels appeared above them and began to sing "Glory to God in the highest and peace on earth to people of good will". Then the angels went back to heaven and the shepherds hurried to see what they had told them. Joseph listened to their story and in his heart he thanked God for the amazing adventure that he was lucky enough to be a part of with Mary and Jesus.

AT THE TEMPLE IN JERUSALEM

Following what the law of Moses tells Jewish parents to do, Joseph and Mary took Jesus to the temple in Jerusalem to present him to the Lord. For the Jews, every first-born son belongs to God: the tradition was to bring the child to the temple and to offer a sacrifice of two doves or pigeons.

In Jerusalem lived a man called Simeon. He was a good and holy man, who loved God more than anything else. The Holy Spirit had revealed to him that he would not die until he had seen the Messiah with his own eyes.

Simeon was already very old but he waited with trust in God.

That day Simeon felt the need to go to the temple. And as soon as he arrived, he saw Joseph and Mary at the entrance and recognized that Jesus was the long-awaited messiah. Simeon took him in his arms and was full of happiness. He began to sing a hymn of praise to God: "My eyes have seen your salvation that you have prepared for all the peoples to see, a light to enlighten the gentiles and to be the glory of your people, Israel."

Nearby was also an old prophetess called Anna. She spent all her time in the temple because of the great love she had for God. When she heard Simeon's words she wanted to see the saviour of the world with her own eyes. She was so happy that she shouted to everyone: "come and see the messiah!" to everyone. Her heart was full of joy.

A TIME IN EGYPT

Joseph was a good and just man, he was generous and brave and was always ready to face any difficulty. He showed this when he obeyed the Angel and once again he had a difficult problem to solve. Jesus's life was in danger, Three Wise Men had come from the East following a star. When they stopped in Jerusalem they spoke with King Herod to ask where they could find the infant King of the Jews. They wanted to know exactly where he would be born.

Herod knew nothing of the birth of the new king and asked the priests and scribes what the scriptures had to say on the matter. They answered that the Messiah would be born in Bethlehem.

The Wise Men wanted to set off immediately, they were in a great hurry to adore the new king and to bring him their precious gifts, but King Herod made them promise to return to him and tell him where they had found the baby. "I also want to go and give homage to the new king" said Herod. This was not true. Herod was jealous of Jesus and did not want him to become king in his place, so he made plans to kill Jesus. But God, who can see into people's hearts, sent a dream to the Wise Men and told them to return home by a different route. Joseph was also warned in a dream that Jesus was in danger. Joseph did not waste any time and left his country to flee to Egypt where Jesus would be safe.

When Herod realised that the Wise Men had tricked him, he was full of anger and ordered that all the children under the age of two in the area of Bethlehem should be killed.

LIFE IN NAZARETH

hen they had been in Egypt for a while, the Angel of the Lord again visited Joseph and told him that Herod was dead. Finally it was safe for Joseph's young family to return to the land of Israel. Joseph led Mary and the young Jesus back to Nazareth, to the house where he had lived before getting married. All his friends and family welcomed them back home. Life continued in Nazareth and when Jesus was eight, Joseph decided that it was time to teach him a trade. He took him to his workshop every day and Jesus followed Joseph everywhere he went. He watched Joseph's every move and asked hundreds of questions. Jesus was happy to be with his earthly father, learning a job that made him feel important!

Joseph loved teaching Jesus everything he knew: the name of each tool, every type of wood, and Jesus helped him to carry things and to saw and sand and plane. Joseph made the most of every chance he had to make Jesus feel useful. The years passed and Jesus was growing up and getting stronger, he was full of wisdom and the hand of God was upon him.

JESUS AMONG THE DOCTORS

Every year Joseph, Mary and Jesus went on a pilgrimage to Jerusalem to celebrate the Passover. It was a long journey and great crowds would travel in caravans together with friends and relatives. Not long after Jesus's twelfth birthday something happened which is the worst fear of many parents and it also made Joseph and Mary very annoyed!

When Passover had ended and it was time to return to Nazareth, Jesus decided to stay behind in Jerusalem without telling his parents!

At the age of 12 Jewish boys were already considered to be adults and were expected to know and to follow the scriptures and the Jewish Law. Jesus had a great love for the faith and he wanted to discuss important questions with the doctors and teachers of the law. The great crowds and caravans were already a day's journey from Jerusalem. When it was time to camp for the night, Mary and Joseph realised that Jesus was not there and even their friends and relatives had not seen him. They were very worried and hurried back to Jerusalem and searched for him for three days. They didn't know what to do. Joseph thought, "Lord God, you entrusted your son to me and now I have lost him!" Mary suggested that they should go to the temple and pray to God to help them find their son.

"Will you send me your angel to help me again?" thought Joseph. When they entered the temple they found Jesus sitting in the midst of all the scribes and teachers who were listening to him with amazement. The boy could answer all their questions with great wisdom even though he was only 12!

19

They looked at each other in disbelief, where did all that wisdom come from?

"Why have you done this to us? Joseph and I were worried sick!" said Mary full of anguish. "Why were you looking for me? Did you not know that I would be in my father's house?" replied Jesus.

Joseph was a man who trusted God and he had recognised God's voice

speaking to him through the Angel. He was always ready to do what God asked him but now he was confused.

Why had Jesus answered like that? What did he mean by those words? Once again Joseph trusted in God and put aside his doubts. He accepted that God would reveal his plan little by little.

IN THE HOUSE OF THE FATHER

Joseph probably died before Jesus began his public ministry. We know this because the Gospels tell us no more about Joseph. When Jesus was on the cross he entrusted his mother to John, the youngest of the twelve apostles. This must have been because she no longer had a husband to look after her.

Just as Joseph looked after Mary, many centuries later, Joseph was proclaimed the protector of the Church. We celebrate his feast on the 19th March.

Joseph is also the patron saint of workers and of carpenters, this is why he is often shown holding a saw or a piece of wood. His feast as St Joseph the Worker is celebrated on the 1st May.

AN INTERESTING FACT

The gospels were written in Greek and the word used to describe Joseph's job is *tekton*. This is much more than a simple carpenter, it was a job that involved all types of woodwork and even stonework and building. In the time of Jesus in Palestine, houses were also made of wood which was then covered with earth and clay.

If your family or someone you know is looking for a new house to live in, St Joseph is the best person to pray to for help. Not only did he build houses for other people but he also provided a house for the Son of God and for the Mother of God.

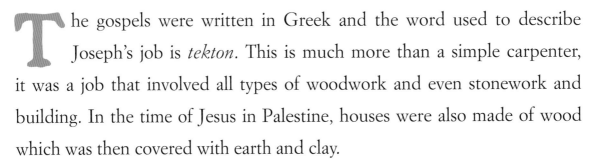

You can pray to him at home or you can often find a statue of St Joseph in church. He is usually shown holding baby Jesus or with a staff with white flowers growing from it. These white flowers remind us of his purity and humility and how much he loved his wife and adopted child, Jesus.

AN IMAGE OF ST JOSEPH

A PRAYER TO ST JOSEPH

St Joseph, holy father of Jesus,
help me to have dreams like yours!
When I am sad
and don't know what to do in my life,
help me to listen to the voice of God
and to be guided by it along the right path.
I do not dream of fame,
or wealth, or power,
I want to dream of my Lord
and stay close to him.